RUMORS OF GOD

EXPERIENCE THE KIND OF FAITH YOU'VE ONLY HEARD ABOUT

DARREN WHITEHEAD & JON TYSON

THOMAS NELSON
Since 1798

NASHVILLE   DALLAS   MEXICO CITY   RIO DE JANEIRO

Published in Nashville, Tennessee, by Thomas Nelson. Thomas Nelson is a registered trademark of Thomas Nelson, Inc.

Thomas Nelson, Inc., titles may be purchased in bulk for educational, business, fund-raising, or sales promotional use. For information, please e-mail SpecialMarkets@ ThomasNelson.com.

Unless otherwise noted, all Scripture verses are taken from HOLY BIBLE: NEW INTERNATIONAL VERSION®. © 1973, 1978, 1984 by International Bible Society. Used by permission of Zondervan Publishing House. All rights reserved.

ISBN: 978-1-4016-7532-5

Printed in the United States of America

12 13 14 15 16 QG 6 5 4 3 2 1

CONTENTS

INTRODUCTION

I have come that they may have life, and have it to the full.
  —John 10:10b

Welcome to a journey that could change your life.

In the Gospel of John, Jesus declared that He came to give His disciples not just life but life "to the full." This phrase, "life to the full," can conjure many thoughts and feelings. What will this life look like? Is such a life available for me today? If it is, why does my everyday experience sometimes seem not very "full"?

If you've ever found yourself asking these questions, you're not alone. Many of us experience a disconnect between the promises of Jesus in the Scriptures and our actual lives. This can produce a growing anxiety in us. We wonder if, maybe, this is as good as our life with God is going to get. Is the exciting time of our faith only present in the past? Are Jesus' promises of a "life to the full" for somebody else and not for us?

These are excellent questions that Darren and Jon address head on in *Rumors of God*. They do so not by simply giving the answers but by asking us to consider the reasons for the answers. Why do we think there is a distance between God's promises and our lives? Where do we imagine that gap comes from and how can we bridge it? This trip will be one of self-reflection and if you are up for that journey, then you are in the right place.

Part of your *Rumors of God* experience will include small group discussion. A small group is an excellent place to process the content of the study, ask questions, and learn from others as you listen to what God is doing in their lives. If you are new to small groups, these can be deeply rewarding times of intimacy and friendship. However, they can also be disastrous. By keeping a few ground rules in mind you'll make this group experience a fruitful one for everybody involved, including you.

First, work to make the group a "safe place." That means being honest about what you're thinking and feeling as well as listening carefully to everyone else. It also means resisting the temptation to "fix" a problem someone might be having and keeping everything your group shares confidential. All this will foster a rewarding sense of community and give God's Spirit a powerful forum to heal you, challenge you, and send you out.

The *Rumors of God* study has the potential to change your life, if you let it. Be honest about where you are struggling and resist the temptation to shut down if the content hits close to home. Examining places where our lives are out of sync is not an invitation to shame but instead a way to open the door to our hearts so God's love can flood in. This is what Jesus wants more than anything, and if we seek this, it is, as he has promised, exactly what we will find.

HOW TO USE THIS GUIDE

Each session includes a DVD clip of Darren and Jon talking about the topic for the session. Following the clip, there will be time for small group discussion. There are lots of questions for use during this time, but you don't have to get through all of them. Focus on the ones that really resonate with your group and go from there.

Your group will also be invited to attempt an Experiment in Truth every session. These experiments are practical undertakings that will put flesh and blood action to the concepts discussed in the video. They are not laws to be followed to avoid punishment but rather opportunities to stretch and grow in the practice of our faith. If you feel that you don't do them right, fall short, or forget, don't worry. The important thing is that you reflect on the process and what you are learning. Keep a notebook or journal with you so you can jot down your thoughts as you attempt each practice. Starting in Session 2, there will be time before watching the DVD to check in with your small group about how last week's experiment went. This will be a great time to listen to others and learn from their experiences. Again, don't worry if you forgot to do the experiment or are just joining the study. Hearing what others have learned will be nourishment enough on its own.

Lastly, each session is concluded with five days of Bible readings and reflection questions called Day by Day. These are an opportunity for you to personally explore the themes from each session and engage in study throughout the week. Do as many or as few as you like. They are a tool, nothing more and nothing less.

Our prayer is that you will enjoy your journey through the *Rumors of God* study and that the God and Father of our Lord Jesus Christ will meet you here and grant you "life to the full."

HOSTAGES OF THE MIND
RUMORS OF ANOTHER DREAM

In his book *Breathing Underwater*, Richard Rhor observes that, "Christians are usually sincere and well-intentioned people until you get to any real issues of ego, control, power, money, pleasure, and security. Then they tend to be pretty much like everybody else."[1] Darren and Jon make this same observation in this first session of *Rumors of God*. They ask us to question what we dream about and then explore where those dreams come from.

This is a risky proposition.

Anytime we allow God to challenge the allegiance we have to false dreams it is threatening. There is a chance we will have to give up something we have been depending on. The question is: Do we trust God to give us something better in return?

As you watch the video, consider what kind of dreams you dream. What informs those dreams? Finally, are you in a place today to be honest about where the inspiration of your dreams lies? God only asks because He wants to bring us freedom, but it is risky to accept the question. Will you trust Him today?

WATCH THE DVD

Play Session 1: *Hostages of the Mind: Rumors of Another Dream*

GROUP DISCUSSION

1. Invite everyone to share their name and answer this question: What is one of the best (or worst) dreams you can remember?

2. Darren and Jon suggest that, underneath it all, Christians' dreams are no different from anyone else's. They say our imaginations have been captured. Do you agree? If so, where do you see evidence of this captivity? If not, why do you disagree?

3. What does Jon mean when he says, "The American story has become our story"? Is it wrong to want a "happy ending" to a story?

4. What is the difference between a dream and a fantasy?

5. What are three things you can imagine that God dreams about?

6. What would it look like for God to release our imaginations? Give an example.

7. What is one practical thing we can do to dream another dream? Brainstorm as a group or reflect as an individual.

EXPERIMENTS IN TRUTH
MEDIA FAST

Rumors of God demonstrates the way marketing has become the dominant force in shaping Christians' imaginations. This week you are invited to take a stand and say no.

At least one day this week try a media fast. Try to spend a day without the influence of TV or computer screens, magazines, or anything that will bring unnecessary advertising into your orbit. Fast from social media sites, print media (like catalogs), and entertainment or news magazines.

The point here is to be intentional, not legalistic. If your work requires a computer screen, make part of your fast abstinence from Facebook. If you have to use your smart phone everyday, pick one evening this week to turn it off overnight. If technology is not your struggle, try wearing clothes that are free of brand logos. We cannot avoid all images, but we can turn down the volume of their messages through our choices and that is the point of this exercise.

Write down your plan here and share it with your study group or a friend before you begin. Ask them if they think your fast is attainable. Then go for it. Keep a notebook with you and write down what you experience to share with the group during the next session. Pay attention to which voices get louder during the fast and which get quieter.

DAY BY DAY

During Session 1 we talked about the way Christians' imaginations are taken over by dreams other than God's. The following devotionals explore this concept further. What makes us dream other dreams? Is this only a recent phenomenon? What resources has God provided for His people to deal with this temptation in the past? What can we learn from our forbearers in faith about liberating our imaginations to hope for God's kingdom to come on earth as it is in heaven?

 # DAY 1

EXODUS 20:17

You shall not covet your neighbor's house. You shall not covet your neighbor's wife, or his male or female servant, his ox or donkey, or anything that belongs to your neighbor.

Read the scripture for today and consider:

✛ How do you define the word "covet"?

✛ Where do you see coveting in our culture today?

The scripture for today is from the Ten Commandments. "Do not covet" is the final command of the ten, yet it is not always easy to pin down what it means. What did God have in mind here? The answer to that question is actually a picture painted by the remainder of the law.

As God laid out the law to the Jewish people, it became clear that He was planning to make them a nation. This meant giving them land, and every Israelite family was promised a particular parcel. This land was a gift from God and everyone was afforded enough land for his or her family to use for their needs. Boundaries around the parcels were to be indicated by short rock walls or boundary stones, which were not to be moved (according to Deut. 19:14). The idea was that God had given everyone enough. All that a family needed could be produced on its parcel. All that was required of each family was to take care of what God had given to them.

The command not to covet in Exodus 20 includes references to spouses, servants, livestock, and property. These are the things that could be seen if you looked over your neighbor's wall to see what was going on in their plot. This is coveting. It's when we peer over the wall and lust for the relationships, property, job, or family of someone else. It's when we want that person's life instead of ours. Such craving can never be slaked and will only produce destruction. It is a foreign dream holding our imaginations captive.

✤ What does coveting what somebody else has say about what God has already given you?

✤ Why is it profitable for a company to create advertising that forces us to covet their products? Have you seen any examples of this recently?

✤ What items are you most likely to covet and why?

 # DAY 2

JAMES 4:2–4

What causes fights and quarrels among you? Don't they come from your desires that battle within you? You desire but do not have, so you kill. You covet but you cannot get what you want, so you quarrel and fight. You do not have because you do not ask God. When you ask, you do not receive, because you ask with wrong motives, that you may spend what you get on your pleasures.

You adulterous people, don't you know that friendship with the world means enmity against God? Therefore, anyone who chooses to be a friend of the world becomes an enemy of God.

Read the scripture for today and consider:

✤ What part of the text do you think relates to the church of today the most?

✤ What part of this letter relates to your life the most? The least?

The letter of James was written to the people of a struggling church. The author challenged their slander, bickering, and deceit, not because they were "breaking the rules" but because they had a job to do. They were the community to whom God chose to demonstrate what He is like to the world. They were the body of Christ, and how they lived mattered.

Look at James 4:2–4 again. It contends that the outgrowth of coveting is violence, and James told his readers that when they asked God for things, they didn't receive them because their motives were improper. And what were their motives? James is quick to tell us: their own pleasures. This sounds very familiar, indeed. Our culture grooms us to be motivated by our own selfish desires. You might say that's just "the way of the world." However, decreeing it as wrong is not good enough. We must also ask how we seek God with right motives.

Jesus said that the law and the prophets could be summed up in two commandments: love God with everything you've got (first) and love your neighbor as yourself (second). Coveting is lusting for what someone else has and that lust motivates us to take what has not been given. Is praying for blessing and provision for others in our community, instead of focusing on ourselves, the antidote for coveting? Is a first step putting the needs of others before our own? Consider how you pray and what you ask for. Is it leading to greater love of God and neighbor, or is that love going somewhere else?

✚ What is the difference between asking God for what you need and asking God for things that will indulge your pleasures?

✚ Verse 3 says that motives matter sometimes. Are there times that motives don't matter when we pray?

✚ What do you think it means to be a "friend of the world and enemy of God"?

 # DAY 3

A prayer of Habakkuk the prophet. On *shigionoth*.
LORD, I have heard of your fame;
  I stand in awe of your deeds, LORD.
Repeat them in our day,
    in our time make them known;
    in wrath remember mercy.

Read the scripture for today and consider:

✤ What do you think the prophet is referring to when he talks about the Lord's "fame" and "deeds"?

✤ What would it look like for God to repeat these deeds in our day? Who would be involved in making this happen?

It has been said that the exodus is the paradigmatic event of the Hebrew Scriptures and the rest of the law and prophets are simply commentary upon it. Repeatedly, God identifies Himself as "the one who brought you out of bondage in Egypt." This makes God's radical, powerful, and definitive rescue of His people from slavery one of the primary ways God wants to be understood. God asks, "Who am I?" and answers, "I am a Rescuer!"

When Habakkuk prophesied, Israel found herself under oppression again. This was a result of her own sin and her exile was understood as God's punishment. Foreign nations ruled her again, yet the cry of the prophet (Hab. 3:1–2) was for God to be who God has always claimed to be—a liberator of the people. It was an appeal for God to act like He did in the Exodus. It was a cry for freedom.

But what if the people don't want to be rescued? What happens if we succeed in achieving the dreams of status, wealth, and power that this world provides? This might actually make God's offer of freedom sound like bad news instead of good news. Jesus found Himself in this situation often. His proclamation of freedom didn't look like what His contemporaries thought it should. Jesus knew the truth and demonstrated that true freedom only comes through sacrifice. This is one of the things He demonstrated on the cross. God's freedom doesn't come in a quick, effortless fix.

✙ What do you spend your time dreaming about?

✤ Do your dreams look like God's dreams? How can you tell?

✤ Is there any part of Jesus' good news proclamation that sounds like bad news to you? Why do you think that is?

 DAY 4

EPHESIANS 3:14–21

For this reason I kneel before the Father, from whom every family in heaven and on earth derives its name. I pray that out of his glorious riches he may strengthen you with power through his Spirit in your inner being, so that Christ may dwell in your hearts through faith. And I pray that you, being rooted and established in love, may have power, together with all the Lord's holy people, to grasp how wide and long and high and deep is the love of Christ, and to know this love that surpasses knowledge—that you may be filled to the measure of all the fullness of God.

Now to him who is able to do immeasurably more than all we ask or imagine, according to his power that is at work within us, to him be glory in the church and in Christ Jesus throughout all generations, for ever and ever! Amen.

Read the scripture for today and consider:

✣ Verse 16 is a prayer for God to strengthen your inner being by the power of the Holy Spirit. Where do you need that today? Take a deep breath and pray.

Verse 20 always reminds me of the movie *Star Wars*. Luke Skywalker tells Han Solo that if he helps rescue the princess he'll receive a reward. When Han asks how much that reward will be, Luke is caught off guard. Unsurely he answers, "Well, more wealth than you can imagine." Han replies, "I don't know. I can imagine quite a bit."[2]

In Ephesians 3:20 the author reminded the community that God can do more than we can imagine. So much more, in fact, that it is beyond measure. This is an impressive and true claim, but it becomes problematic if our dreams are all about us. In a consumer society we are taught over and over again that our needs are all that matter. We get used to dreaming about great things for ourselves and, when those things do not materialize, we are disappointed and can even become cynical and bitter. We even extend that disappointment to God because "Ephesians 3:20 says God will do even more than we can ask or imagine. So why didn't my dreams come true?"

The answer is in verse 21. The immeasurable activity of God works towards God's glory, not simply ours. To be sure, God is glorified when our lives manifest healing, joy, beauty, and hope. God wants us to be whole. However, God wants much more than this as well. God's mission in Jesus encompasses the whole cosmos. Even the best things we can say about God's goodness and love will fall short of how good and loving God really is. He is truly better than we can ever imagine! This is what Ephesians invites us to do. Give up our culture's dreams of money, sex, and power and embrace Jesus' revolution of faith, hope, and love.

✤ When you hear the phrase "God's dreams," what does it make you think of?

✛ Take a moment and imagine. What are the most outrageous, hopeful, beautiful, and redemptive things you can imagine God doing in your lifetime? Write these down.

✛ Take a moment and pray for each of the things you listed in the question above. Ask God what part you can play in making each of these dreams come true. Finally, be quiet and listen.

 # DAY 5

PSALM 104:27–33

All creatures look to you
    to give them their food at the proper time.
When you give it to them,
    they gather it up;
when you open your hand,
    they are satisfied with good things.
When you hide your face,
    they are terrified;
when you take away their breath,
    they die and return to the dust.
When you send your Spirit,
    they are created,
    and you renew the face of the ground.
May the glory of the LORD endure forever;
    may the LORD rejoice in his works—
he who looks at the earth, and it trembles,
    who touches the mountains, and they smoke.
I will sing to the LORD all my life;
I will sing praise to my God as long as I live.

Read the scripture for today and consider:

✚ When was the last time you were satisfied? What brought about that satisfaction?

✚ Verses 27–28 say God satisfies all creatures with good things. Have you ever been satisfied by something that wasn't good for you? Why did you answer the way you did?

Even though the majority of world's resources flow into the United States, we still fear there is not enough. We live by a myth of scarcity. This myth says there may not be adequate provision for all, so you must take what you can while you can. It assumes that you will not be given what you need—so you must seize it instead. This is the only way to ensure that *you* have what you want.

The problem with this myth is that it is in direct contradiction with today's psalm. Psalm 104 is a commentary on Genesis 1, and Genesis 1 is all about abundance. In fact, things were so abundant and teeming with plenty in Genesis 1 that on the seventh day, God chose to take a break. You can almost imagine God saying, "I just need some downtime here!" Creation is full of everything we need and the psalm today celebrates that. We are reminded that God not only gives food to all in the proper time but also gives the very breath that sustains the earth. Everything the creation needs flows as a gift from the Creator, which means nothing can be taken, only received.

The psalm challenges us to consider which story we believe: God's creation of plenty or our culture's myth of scarcity. The choice is not easy, because the mouthpiece of the myth of scarcity is everywhere. We see numerous advertising images a day telling us that we don't have enough and that we need more of what we do have. Still, God's invitation is to listen to the truth rather than the lies. God has enough for you. Will you believe it?

✢ Do you agree that we live by a "myth of scarcity" in the United States? If so, where have you seen this myth? If not, why not?

✤ What kinds of behaviors would flow out of people who live by the myth of scarcity? What about those who live out of the creation of abundance?

✤ Do you trust that God has enough for you? Why or why not? What makes that hard to believe? What makes it easy?

THE GREAT REVERSAL
RUMORS OF GENEROSITY

When Jesus described the kingdom of God to His first century audience, many were confused. They had preconceived ideas about what God's rule and reign would look like when it came flooding into their world, and whatever Jesus was talking about did not fit. For Jesus, the kingdom was about reversals and surprises. It was a place where the last would be first and the first would be last. It was a place where the greatest would be a servant of all. It was a place where God's favor and love could not be earned, only received. It was a place where forgiveness overturned revenge, and power was demonstrated in weakness. In short, the kingdom Jesus announced was upside down and backward from the way the world "normally" worked. And the same thing is true today.

We live in a culture that defines success in terms of material gain, power, and status. Yet for all the wealth and technology the West has generated, we are more greedy, lonely, and unhappy than ever. This system is not working and yet we feel the allure of its promises. We think, "Maybe it will work for me," and we go on pursuing whatever is newer and better.

Jesus offers us another way to live.

What if the gateway to a genuinely godly life is not in getting more but in giving more? What if we were created to share more than to hold? What if the way this world "normally" works when it comes to our resources is broken and backward? And what if generosity, even radical generosity, is the gateway to getting our hearts back and embarking in lives worth living?

CHECKING IN

Last week's experiment was a media fast. Invite people from the group to share their experiences. Explore:

✤ Was anything difficult about the fast? Was anything easy?

✤ Did anything seem to "call for you" more loudly once you determined to give it up for the day? What did you learn by denying it?

✛ Did anyone have a bad experience with the fast? Why was it bad or difficult?

WATCH THE DVD

Play Session 2: *The Great Reversal: Rumors of Generosity*

GROUP DISCUSSION

1. What is one of the most significant gifts you have ever been given?

2. What is the "silver medal syndrome" the guys mention? Is there anywhere you see it in your own life?

3. Planned and perceived obsolescence—do you experience this? How does it make you feel?

4. Our whole cultural rhythm is work, watch, and spend. Do you agree that it's toxic to our faith?

5. Jon says that we have reversed the Christian teaching "to live is Christ and to die is gain" and made it "to live is gain and to die is Christ." Do you think that's true? Why or why not?

6. Darren and Jon explain the difference between work, rent, royalties, and privilege. Do you see these differences? Are they fair? Do you recognize your own economics on this scale?

7. Darren says that Jesus invites us to give away our privilege. What is a healthy example of this kind of sacrifice? What is an unhealthy version of this kind of sacrifice?

8. Brainstorm as a group or reflect as an individual: What is one practical thing we can do to make the rumors of generosity come true in our lives?

EXPERIMENTS IN TRUTH
"GIVE TO ANY WHO ASK OF YOU"

Generosity is not something that happens by accident in a person's life. It is the result of intent and practice, and that is what we are going to do this week.

In Matthew 5:42 Jesus said, "Give to the one who asks you, and do not turn away from the one who wants to borrow from you." This is your experiment this week. For one whole day, give to anyone who asks of you. Be it a panhandler asking for spare change or your roommate looking for the remote control, if it is within your power, say yes. As you engage this practice, pay attention to what happens. How does God meet you and who does He bring your way? What do you learn about generosity and living open-handedly? It may not always be possible to say yes, but do your best and bring a notebook along so you can jot down some of your experiences. People will want to hear them next week.

DAY BY DAY

Rumors of God explores what generosity looks like when it takes root in many areas of our lives. This week's daily reflections center specifically on our relationship to money. Each day takes a piece of the biblical witness and investigates what its implications are for people of God who want to live generously.

 # DAY I

DEUTERONOMY 8:10–18

When you have eaten and are satisfied, praise the LORD your God for the good land he has given you. Be careful that you do not forget the LORD your God, failing to observe his commands, his laws and his decrees that I am giving you this day. Otherwise, when you eat and are satisfied, when you build fine houses and settle down, and when your herds and flocks grow large and your silver and gold increase and all you have is multiplied, then your heart will become proud and you will forget the LORD your God, who brought you out of Egypt, out of the land of slavery. He led you through the vast and dreadful wilderness, that thirsty and waterless land, with its venomous snakes and scorpions. He brought you water out of hard rock. He gave you manna to eat in the wilderness, something your ancestors had never known, to humble and test you so that in the end it might go well with you. You may say to yourself, "My power and the strength of my hands have produced this wealth for me." But remember the LORD your God, for it is he who gives you the ability to produce wealth, and so confirms his covenant, which he swore to your ancestors, as it is today.

Read the scripture for today and consider:

✤ What stuck out to you from the reading today?

✤ Deuteronomy draws a connection between being satisfied and being selfish. Do you think that connection is real? Why or why not?

Why is money such an alluring thing? Is it because we want to buy whatever our hearts desire? Partly. Is it because we feel compelled to "keep up with the Joneses" and want to show to our neighbors that we are getting our "piece of the pie"? Perhaps. Is it because we think it will solve whatever problem is causing anxiety in the moment? Possibly.

However, the deeper reason that money is alluring is its promise of control. If we have means at our disposal, we believe we can affect our will in our lives and the world. We imagine that enough money will allow us to call all the shots in our lives and will provide us security and comfort.

This is precisely what puts money in competition with God sometimes and why Yahweh warned the people of Israel about the dangers of prosperity. In Deuteronomy 8 God cautioned the people to stick close to His way when the bounty of their new life in the land rolled in. Otherwise, He said, they would be tempted to forget God and take the credit for His great gift of wealth themselves. This is not a warning that God will be grumpy if His people are ungrateful. It is a warning that seeking money for security and control will ruin them.

In verse 18 God reminded them that He gave them even the ability to produce wealth. There was nothing they had that did not come from God. He would care for them. The question was, would they trust Him to do so? The same question is put to us. Will we trust God for our security and provision? Or are we tempted to leave God behind when times are good?

✤ Do you agree that money is tempting because it offers control? Why or why not?

✤ How do you see money competing with God in our day?

✤ What part of your life is easy to entrust to God?

✤ What part of your life is more difficult to trust Him with?

 DAY 2

Someone in the crowd said to him, "Teacher, tell my brother to divide the inheritance with me."

Jesus replied, "Man, who appointed me a judge or an arbiter between you?" Then he said to them, "Watch out! Be on your guard against all kinds of greed; life does not consist in an abundance of possessions."

And he told them this parable: "The ground of a certain rich man yielded an abundant harvest. He thought to himself, 'What shall I do? I have no place to store my crops.'

"Then he said, 'This is what I'll do. I will tear down my barns and build bigger ones, and there I will store my surplus grain. And I'll say to myself, "You have plenty of grain laid up for many years. Take life easy; eat, drink and be merry."'

"But God said to him, 'You fool! This very night your life will be demanded from you. Then who will get what you have prepared for yourself?'

"This is how it will be with whoever stores up things for themselves but is not rich toward God."

Read the scripture for today and consider:

✦ What stuck out to you from the reading?

✤ Jesus says, "Life does not consist in an abundance of possessions." What do you think it consists of then?

When a rabbi would tell a parable the point was to implicate the listeners. The teacher wanted to see if they both understood the parable and could learn something from the characters' mistakes or successes. This question at the end of a parable was will the audience act on what they now know?[3]

With this in mind, reread today's passage. In response to a family squabble about property and wealth (something he was licensed to arbitrate as a rabbi), the rabbi tells a story about a man who became fabulously wealthy. This wealth has come to him through an abundant crop (something that is a gift) and yields more than he can ever consume. What will he do? He needs a plan, so he consults . . . only himself (v. 17). This is an ancient, Near Eastern way of pointing out that the man is utterly alone. He has no family. No friends. His wealth has isolated him to the point that he has lost sight of what a life is supposed to consist of. When he does settle on a plan, it consists of taking the surplus, building bigger barns, and storing it all up for himself so he can "take life easy." God calls this "foolish" because He knows that the man is going to die that night. So what will have been the point of seeking a life on easy street?

What will we take away from this parable today? Have we heard and have we heard?

✤ Do you think the rich man's choices were foolish? Why or why not?

✤ Do you think it is wrong to save money for the future? Why or why not?

✙ Is there anything we can learn from this story about the way we should manage our money and resources today?

 # DAY 3

LUKE 16:1–13

Jesus told his disciples: "There was a rich man whose manager was accused of wasting his possessions. So he called him in and asked him, 'What is this I hear about you? Give an account of your management, because you cannot be manager any longer.'

"The manager said to himself, 'What shall I do now? My master is taking away my job. I'm not strong enough to dig, and I'm ashamed to beg—I know what I'll do so that, when I lose my job here, people will welcome me into their houses.'

"So he called in each one of his master's debtors. He asked the first, 'How much do you owe my master?'

"'Nine hundred gallons of olive oil,' he replied.

"The manager told him, 'Take your bill, sit down quickly, and make it four hundred and fifty.'

"Then he asked the second, 'And how much do you owe?'

"'A thousand bushels of wheat,' he replied.

"He told him, 'Take your bill and make it eight hundred.'

"The master commended the dishonest manager because he had acted shrewdly. For the people of this world are more shrewd in dealing with their own kind than are the people of the light. I tell you, use worldly wealth to gain friends for yourselves, so that when it is gone, you will be welcomed into eternal dwellings.

"Whoever can be trusted with very little can also be trusted with much, and whoever is dishonest with very little will also be dishonest with much. So if you have not been trustworthy in handling worldly wealth, who will trust you with true riches? And if you have not been trustworthy with someone else's property, who will give you property of your own?

"No one can serve two masters. Either you will hate the one and love the other, or you will be devoted to the one and despise the other. You cannot serve both God and money."

Read the scripture for today and consider:

✤ What do you think the point of this parable is in your own words?

The parable of the shrewd manager is a brilliant yet tricky parable. It is tricky because at first blush it sounds like Jesus is praising someone for being dishonest at their job. Is this what's going on? No. What is going on is that Jesus is offering a powerful lesson on the purpose of money.

The parable opens with a manager who has been fired because his boss (a wealthy landowner) thinks he is wasting company resources. Whether this is true or not, we don't know. What we do know is that the manager is worried. He has had a cushy life working for the landowner and now that he has been fired, he is worried about finding another job. How can he use this situation to save face and position himself to have some kind of future stability?

The landowner has sent the manager to close out his accounts and turn in the books as his final act of business. However, what he does is brilliant. When each of the landowner's customers shows up, the manager cuts them a great deal. Slashing what they owed the landowner, sometimes, in half. Then, when the manager returns and presents the books to his boss, he is commended! How can this be? It would seem the landowner had been overcharging his clients to avoid certain tax codes and Torah regulations. By cutting the deals that he did, the manager makes his boss look extremely generous while simultaneously bringing him into alignment with God's law. This was actually a win-win situation and curried favor for the manager with each of the landowner's clients. This manager figured out how to use money to gain friends for himself.

This is the point. Money, says Jesus, is a tool. It can be used to build something that will not last (profits, empires, and bank accounts) or it can be used to build something that will last (friendships). Our relationships with God and with one another will last in the new Creation. They matter now and after we die. They are our true riches.

✜ Jesus says you cannot serve God and money. What does that mean to you?

✜ How can you use your money to build things into God's new world that will last?

 DAY 4

I TIMOTHY 6:6–10

But godliness with contentment is great gain. For we brought nothing into the world, and we can take nothing out of it. But if we have food and clothing, we will be content with that. Those who want to get rich fall into temptation and a trap and into many foolish and harmful desires that plunge people into ruin and destruction. For the love of money is a root of all kinds of evil. Some people, eager for money, have wandered from the faith and pierced themselves with many griefs.

Read the scripture for today and consider:

✦ Verse 9 says that those who want to get rich fall into "foolish and harmful desires that plunge people into destruction." Do you agree? If so, what do you think some of those desires are? If not, why don't you agree?

Sometimes it is easy to forget that documents such as 1 Timothy are actually letters. Before they were part of the Christian Bible they were correspondence written to particular communities and leaders for the building up of their lives and ministries. As such, we have to remember that when we encounter these texts we are reading somebody else's mail. We have only one end of a conversation and can only imagine what the other side is like. It is precisely this sort of imagining you are invited to do today.

First Timothy was written to a church leader about how to take care of the community he had been entrusted with. Money, in particular the desire to get rich, seemed to be a force of darkness in this church's life. What do you think was going in on the life of this community that would provoke such a response in the letter? Do you think the author of 1 Timothy was referencing anything or anyone in particular when he mentioned those who had wandered from the faith, eager for money? What kinds of "griefs" do you think they might have pierced themselves with? Take a moment to wonder and imagine. Can you think of situations in which the church might need to hear this today?

❖ The church in 1 Timothy was struggling with the pursuit of wealth. Do you think the church today struggles with the same thing? Where do you see that struggle manifest itself?

❖ Verse 6 says that if we have food and clothes we should find contentment with that. Would you be satisfied if your food and clothing was provided for but you had to give up other pursuits? Why or why not? What causes you anxiety at the thought of giving it up?

 DAY 5

ECCLESIASTES 5:10–12

Whoever loves money never has enough;

whoever loves wealth is never satisfied with their income.

This too is meaningless.

As goods increase,

so do those who consume them.

And what benefit are they to the owners

except to feast their eyes on them?

The sleep of a laborer is sweet,

whether they eat little or much,

but as for the rich, their abundance

permits them no sleep.

Read the scripture for today and consider:

✤ Ecclesiastes is a kind of literature called "wisdom literature." Does any part of the proverb sound wise to you?

✤ What does this piece of wisdom stir up in you when you read it?

Ecclesiastes suggests that there is a cycle to accumulating wealth. It begins when we succeed a little in gaining the riches we seek and then snowballs into the angst of never having enough. The proverb suggests that not only is there no benefit to accumulating "stuff," the act itself is in fact meaningless. It is the essence of a chaotic, pointless existence that produces sleepless nights and increases anxiety.

How then should we live in regard to our things? One answer is through the rhythm of generosity. All we have comes from God. It is a gift. Just as we suggested on Day 1 of this week, our job is simply to care for what has been given to us. This is called stewardship, and it means all of our resources, including money, really belong to someone else. Our responsibility is to get it where the rightful owner wants it to go.

Such a perspective frees us from clinging too tightly to the resources that come our way. If we hold them with an open hand, we start to recognize the privilege it is to partner with God in providing for His creation. This way of generosity is also a way of peace. It is the way of life that grows truth, beauty, and justice and makes our lives rich with meaning and purpose. All that is required is that we say yes to God's invitation to follow where He leads.

✤ What are some things that are hard for you to hold with an open hand?

✤ Is there a place in your life where generosity comes easily to you? If so, where?

✤ Is there a place in your life where it is hard to be generous?

✤ Do you agree that generosity will lead to peace?

GETTING THE GOSPEL IN ORDER

T his session is about grace. Grace is a tricky topic because it is often confused with mercy. Mercy, with all its generous and forgiving release, is a wonderful part of God's character, but grace is something more.

The difference is captured in U2's song "Grace." The last verse of the song goes like this:

> *What once was hurt*
> *What once was friction*
> *What left a mark*
> *No longer stings*
> *Because grace makes beauty*
> *Out of ugly things*

What the song captures is the way that grace does more than let someone off the hook. Grace changes things. Grace restores. Grace takes what was once ugly in our bodies, hearts, and minds and makes it beautiful. God's transforming grace is active and it is also free. That may be the hardest part to accept.

Religion, not Jesus, teaches us that we must work to earn favor from our God. Jesus offers grace, free of charge, and all we have to do is accept it. This is easier said than done. Many of us still want Jesus to work like religion. We want to earn His grace and favor, but we can't because we cannot earn what we already have. The question is, will you accept this gift?

This week, consider what you think of grace. How do you define it? What is your experience of it? And finally, what, if any, are the barriers you may have to giving and receiving it? It is offered freely. All we have to do is receive it.

CHECKING IN

Last week's experiment in truth was called "Give to any who ask of you." In this experiment participants were invited to spend one day saying yes to as many requests as they could, no matter how large or small. Reflect personally or with a group:

✠ What is one story that stands out from your day of generosity?

✚ Who came your way asking for things?

✚ Was it easier to give to some people than others? If yes, why do you think that was?

✚ What did you learn about generosity and living open-handedly?

WATCH THE DVD

Play Session 3: *Getting the Gospel in Order: Rumors of Grace*

GROUP DISCUSSION

1. If you had to pick two words to describe *grace,* what would they be?

2. The guys open the video this week with a quote from C. S. Lewis that says Christianity's distinction among world religions is its grace. However, they contend, if we did a survey today, most people would say that Christianity's distinction is that it is judgmental. Do you think they are right? Why or why not?

3. Recount Darren's credit card and bank account analogy to show the distinction between mercy and grace. What's so wrong with confusing these two?

4. The guys say that grace is not about letting people off the hook for offenses. Instead it's about lavishing them with extravagant gifts of love. Is it easier for you to show mercy or grace?

5. Can someone show grace without condoning sin? How?

6. How does Jon's "poo story" illustrate what grace is?

7. Do you ever feel like you need to earn God's grace? Why is that? Is that the message of the gospel?

8. Brainstorm as a group a few ways we can train to get better at giving and receiving grace.

EXPERIMENTS IN TRUTH
THE JESUS PRAYER

Rumors of God says that the Rosetta Stone to the gospel is understanding the grace and love of Jesus in spite of our personal sin. The experiment this week invites participants to engage this claim.

One of the cornerstones of personal devotion in the Eastern Orthodox Church is called "The Jesus Prayer." The Jesus Prayer is an ancient prayer taken from the teachings of early Christians who lived in the desert. It is a simple phrase that goes like this:

Lord Jesus Christ, Son of God, have mercy on me a sinner.

The prayer invites the one who prays it to approach Jesus and call out to Him from a place of humility. This humility is not anchored in shame but in confidence that Jesus loves us and has redeemed us.

The Jesus Prayer is prayed by repetition as you breathe. As you inhale say to yourself, "Lord Jesus Christ, Son of God." Then, as you exhale say, "Have mercy on me a sinner." Try praying the prayer twenty times a day this week. Pay attention to what happens before and after you pray it. See if it comes to your mind to pray the prayer while you are on the go this week. How might this prayer become a companion instead of a duty?

DAY BY DAY

The session and the readings this week focused on the grace and mercy of Jesus' gospel. What is the nature of God's grace? What can we learn from the way it is offered and actualized in the Bible?

 ## DAY 1

1 JOHN 1:8–10

If we claim to be without sin, we deceive ourselves and the truth is not in us. If we confess our sins, he is faithful and just and will forgive us our sins and purify us from all unrighteousness. If we claim we have not sinned, we make him out to be a liar and his word is not in us.

Read the scripture for today and consider:

✤ What circumstances do you think prompted the author of 1 John to write the passage above?

✤ Is the scenario you imagined one that could be true for the church today?

Sin is a tricky topic to address because, when it comes up, many people feel immediately shamed. Facing our faults can be difficult and painful, but God's desire is not for us to wallow in a place of shame in regard to our sin. God wants to set us free.

The passage from 1 John today has strong language in it. It says that anyone who denies their sin is "deceived" and is also calling God a "liar." However, the point of this text is not to try to bully someone into humility. Instead, it is coming from the perspective that God's desire is freedom and wholeness for every human being He has made. However, if any of those people claim they do not need to be rescued, then they are cutting themselves off from God's freeing activity (or at least making it really hard for God to do.)

This passage of Scripture is an invitation to join God in our healing, even as He heals the whole creation. When we are honest about our brokenness and sin, God will forgive, heal, and restore us just as He is healing and restoring all things. However, if we claim that we have no sin, then although God's offer still stands, it will go unaccepted. It's as if we are telling God that He's trying to solve a problem we don't have, so thanks but no thanks.

The vulnerability and risk involved in being honest about our brokenness is not trivial. This is a real source of fear in many of our lives, but it doesn't have to be. Being real and honest about our struggles in the presence of God and the presence of our neighbors can radically heal us. Such healing enables us to be effective partners with God in not only our own healing but in His healing of everything else.

✛ On a scale of 1–10, with 1 being not scary and 10 being terrifying, how scary is it for you to be honest about your sin?

✛ Have you ever had an experience in which you were vulnerable with someone about a weakness and they accepted you anyway? When was that?

 DAY 2

ACTS 15:5–11

Then some of the believers who belonged to the party of the Pharisees stood up and said, "The Gentiles must be circumcised and required to keep the law of Moses."

The apostles and elders met to consider this question. After much discussion, Peter got up and addressed them: "Brothers, you know that some time ago God made a choice among you that the Gentiles might hear from my lips the message of the gospel and believe. God, who knows the heart, showed that he accepted them by giving the Holy Spirit to them, just as he did to us. He did not discriminate between us and them, for he purified their hearts by faith. Now then, why do you try to test God by putting on the necks of Gentiles a yoke that neither we nor our ancestors have been able to bear? No! We believe it is through the grace of our Lord Jesus that we are saved, just as they are."

Read the scripture for today and consider:

✤ Did anything stick out to you as you read the passage? If so, what?

The passage for today is from the book of Acts. It is an excerpt from a larger moment in the life of the church called the Jerusalem Council. This was the meeting where the emerging church of the first century came together to decide if Gentile believers could be Christians without having to convert to Judaism first.

The consequences of the decision seemed huge to the believers of the day. If it were true that God accepted Gentiles outside of their adherence to the Mosaic covenant, it would seem to overturn thousands of years of tradition. Yet Peter's experience at the house of Cornelius the Centurion (v. 7) suggested that God was up to something new. The mark of membership in the family of God was not circumcision but instead the giving and receiving of the Holy Spirit. Furthermore, the giving of the Spirit was a gift. No one earned it. It came simply through God's grace.

This is the conclusion the church comes to in Acts 15 and the reality we must wrestle with today. Can we earn God's rescue, love, and care or is it simply a gift to be received? If the former is the case, then Jesus' gospel is not good news at all. It is just more rules to be kept to earn a deity's favor. However, if the latter is the case and God's love is free and need only be received, we must ask whether or not we will receive it. What will you choose today? Will you accept what's been offered to you?

✤ Has your experience of Christianity been one in which God's love and rescue was given freely, or does it have to be earned?

✤ Is it easy or hard for you to receive gifts? Explain your answer.

✤ Does it sound like good news to hear that God is already on your side and extends new life to you? Why or why not?

DAY 3

As for you, you were dead in your transgressions and sins, in which you used to live when you followed the ways of this world and of the ruler of the kingdom of the air, the spirit who is now at work in those who are disobedient. All of us also lived among them at one time, gratifying the cravings of our flesh and following its desires and thoughts. Like the rest, we were by nature deserving of wrath. But because of his great love for us, God, who is rich in mercy, made us alive with Christ even when we were dead in transgressions—it is by grace you have been saved. And God raised us up with Christ and seated us with him in the heavenly realms in Christ Jesus, in order that in the coming ages he might show the incomparable riches of his grace, expressed in his kindness to us in Christ Jesus. For it is by grace you have been saved, through faith—and this is not from yourselves, it is the gift of God—not by works, so that no one can boast. For we are God's handiwork, created in Christ Jesus to do good works, which God prepared in advance for us to do.

Read the scripture for today and consider:

✤ How does this passage sound to you today? Is it good news or bad news?

✤ Why did you answer the way you did?

Ephesians is another New Testament letter in which we only have one side of the correspondence. However, it seems clear from today's passage that the community this was written to needed a reminder that bragging about their holiness is not part of God's kingdom. Salvation is given by God as a direct expression of love. Therefore, it is offered with kindness and cannot be earned. The Ephesians started out in the same sinking ship of sin and powerlessness and when they were pulled to safety and restored by Jesus it was because of nothing they did. This is good news but begs the question—now what? Now that rescue has come, what do we do next?

Ephesians 2:10 answers this question.

We were created to "do good works." Part of God's purpose in creating human beings was for them to act on God's behalf in the creation. The same is true today. The church will demonstrate the truth of God's salvation in Jesus, in part through the way they act in their communities. God's salvation has a purpose. We are rescued, restored, and set free in order to join God in the renewal of all things. So now the question is, what are you going to do?

✚ The Ephesians' old way of life is described as one of "gratifying the cravings of our flesh and following its desires and thoughts." What do you think this way of life looks like?

✚ Do you relate to it?

✛ What are some of the "good works" that you might be called to join God in doing? (List three.)

 ## DAY 4

ACTS 2:42–47

They devoted themselves to the apostles' teaching and to fellowship, to the breaking of bread and to prayer. Everyone was filled with awe at the many wonders and signs performed by the apostles. All the believers were together and had everything in common. They sold property and possessions to give to anyone who had need. Every day they continued to meet together in the temple courts. They broke bread in their homes and ate together with glad and sincere hearts, praising God and enjoying the favor of all the people. And the Lord added to their number daily those who were being saved.

✛ Do you think people today have a generally positive or a generally negative view of the church?

✤ Why do you think the early church in Acts enjoyed the "favor of all people"?

Yesterday we asked the question, When God acts to save us and we accept it, then what? Ephesians 2:10 declared that we were created to do good works, but what does that look like in practice?

In the passage from Acts 2, we get a description of the life of the early church. These were some of the first responders to Jesus' gospel invitation of grace and mercy. Look at the way it manifested itself in their lives. They were radically generous, selling their own property and possessions to give to the needy. They devoted themselves to the teaching of the disciples, meeting together, sharing meals, and praying. They eschewed private ownership of their things and opted to view their possessions as community property.

The grace of God came to these people and one of their responses was radical generosity. What about us? How have we responded to Jesus' gospel invitation? Will we let God's grace manifest itself in our lives as action?

✤ How does God's love and grace manifest itself in your actions?

✤ Do we have the same kind of generosity as the early church in our own lives?

✤ What makes this kind of generosity easy? What makes it difficult?

✤ What are other examples of faith-in-action that you have witnessed in your own life or the lives of others?

 DAY 5

PSALM 98

Sing to the LORD a new song,
    for he has done marvelous things;
his right hand and his holy arm
    have worked salvation for him.
The LORD has made his salvation known
    and revealed his righteousness to the nations.
He has remembered his love
    and his faithfulness to Israel;
all the ends of the earth have seen
    the salvation of our God.
Shout for joy to the LORD, all the earth,
    burst into jubilant song with music;
make music to the LORD with the harp,
    with the harp and the sound of singing,
with trumpets and the blast of the ram's horn—
    shout for joy before the LORD, the King.
Let the sea resound, and everything in it,
    the world, and all who live in it.
Let the rivers clap their hands,
    let the mountains sing together for joy;
let them sing before the LORD,
    for he comes to judge the earth.
He will judge the world in righteousness
    and the peoples with equity.

Read the scripture for today and consider:

✛ This is a psalm of exuberant praise to God. According to the psalm, what is God going to do that is so good and exciting?

Psalm 98 is a powerful song of praise to God. It begins with a call to write new songs to God, the Saving One. This points back to Israel's salvation from slavery in Egypt and also looks forward, suggesting that what God is going to do is even better than Israel's deliverance. In fact, it is so good that the old songs about God's goodness are not sufficient. New songs must be composed.

From there, the psalm crescendos with dramatic descriptions of a party that is breaking out across the entire earth in anticipation of what this saving God is going to do. Shouts of joy will be followed by new songs and trumpet blasts. This will be followed by the creation itself (the sea, rivers, mountains, and all their inhabitants) all joining this party to cheer what God is going to do. What could this be? What could be such good news that the whole creation is vibrating with celebration?

God is coming to judge the earth (v. 9).

This almost seems like an oxymoron, but it is not. To the Hebrew people God's judgment was actually a good thing. It was something to both anticipate and celebrate. This is because the Jews understood God's judgment as the time when He would right the wrong in the world. This was the time that God's justice would flow and the broken things of this world would be put back together and made new.

Rumors of God suggests that Christians are known by their judgment, but it's the wrong kind of judgment. When God judges He will call evil, wrong, and goodness "right" with the objective of healing a broken world. In this way God's judgment is good news indeed.

✤ Do you think of God's judgment as something positive or negative? Why did you answer the way you did?

✤ What can Christians today learn from God's kind of judgment when they speak about what is right and wrong in their world?

GIVING UP YOUR RIGHTS
RUMORS OF FORGIVENESS

In his watershed book *Mere Christianity*, C. S. Lewis states, "Forgiveness is a lovely idea until you have someone to forgive."[4] This quote has endured because of its truth and power. Most people know that forgiveness is beautiful, redemptive, and even necessary, yet they struggle to find ways to actually forgive. This struggle is common but not without consequence.

Jesus teaches that forgiving others and being forgiven by God go hand in hand. In Matthew 6:14–15 (a scripture you are invited to consider further on Day 5 of the readings this week) Jesus says that if you forgive others their sins you too will be forgiven, yet if you don't forgive others their sins yours will not be forgiven by God either. What is this all about? Why would this God, who is fundamentally defined by the way He gives unmerited grace and mercy, suddenly get so conditional about everything?

One answer is that Jesus is not taking a left turn from His offer of grace that is free of charge. Instead, He is simply describing the way things work. It seems that human beings are made with the capacity to both give and receive forgiveness. However, the giving and receiving flow through the same channel. So if we close down our offering of forgiveness to others, we will subsequently close down the path through which we can receive forgiveness as well. It's like a snorkel. The air we inhale and exhale all flows through the same tube. It is with our hearts that we give and receive forgiveness.

As you participate in this session, consider how you approach forgiveness. Is your heart open or closed to forgiving others? Also consider how your posture in regard to forgiveness might affect your relationship with God. His desire is to lavish us with love and forgiveness. The question for us is, will we be open to receive it?

CHECKING IN

Last week's experiment in truth was to pray the Jesus Prayer, "Lord Jesus Christ, Son of God, have mercy on me a sinner," twenty times a day. Reflect personally or with a group:

✦ Was praying the Jesus Prayer a positive or negative experience for you? Explain your answer.

✦ Where did you pray the prayer? Why did you choose the space you did?

✦ In the famous 19th century Russian work, *The Way of the Pilgrim*, the main character says that he prayed the prayer so much it started to wake him up in the morning.[5] Did you have any experiences in which the prayer came to mind in ways that surprised you?

✦ Was naming yourself "a sinner" during the prayer a helpful practice? Why or why not?

WATCH THE DVD

Play Session 4: *Giving Up Your Rights: Rumors of Forgiveness*

GROUP DISCUSSION

1. What stuck out to you the most from this week's video?

2. Darren shares a story about Simon, who, after years of abuse and mistreatment, decides that he hates his father and wants only pain and suffering for him. Do you relate to this feeling at all? Is there anyone you want bad things to happen to because of things they have done?

3. The guys suggest that forgiveness is hard to do. Do you agree? Why or why not?

4. The guys liken God's forgiveness of Assyria in Jonah to God's showing mercy and grace to Hitler. How does that make you feel? Who is the "Assyria" of our day?

5. Is there anyone who is beyond forgiveness? Why or why not?

6. Is it true that when we forgive people we are often the ones set free? Why or why not?

7. The guys list six myths of forgiveness.

    • *Forgiveness is the same as forgetting.*

    • *Forgiveness is the same as reconciliation.*

    • *Forgiveness is the same as excusing the offense.*

    • *Forgiveness is weak and not strong.*

• *Forgiveness is a simple decision instead of a process.*

• *Forgiveness is contingent on the perpetrator admitting he or she is wrong.*

Which of these myths is the hardest for you to let go of?

8. What are some practical steps you can take this week to open your heart and receive God's forgiveness so that you can then extend it to others?

EXPERIMENTS IN TRUTH
PRAY FOR THOSE WHO PERSECUTE YOU

In Luke 6:27–31 Jesus teaches that His disciples are to love their enemies and pray for those who persecute them. What does this mean in practice?

Take a piece of paper and, prayerfully, write down the name of one person you consider an enemy. This can be someone who has hurt you, broken your trust, let you down, or whom you just plain struggle to forgive. Attach the piece of paper somewhere you will see it every day (a bathroom mirror, dashboard of your car, etc.). Every time you see that person's name this week, pray a blessing on that person. This is not the same thing as forgiveness or reconciliation. This is simply an attempt to open your heart to what it means to love and be at peace with God and neighbors. Pay attention to what you experience during this exercise and jot it down to share with the group next week.

DAY BY DAY

Rumors of God explores the wonders and challenges of forgiveness. This week's readings explore the practicalities.

 DAY I

MATTHEW 18:15–17

If your brother or sister sins, go and point out their fault, just between the two of you. If they listen to you, you have won them over. But if they will not listen, take one or two others along, so that "every matter may be established by the testimony of two or three witnesses." If they still refuse to listen, tell it to the church; and if they refuse to listen even to the church, treat them as you would a pagan or a tax collector.

Read the scripture for today and consider:

✠ Which part of Jesus' teaching seems the most challenging to put into practice? Why?

In Matthew 18 Jesus was teaching His disciples how to implement the kingdom rhythms of forgiveness into their common lives. His teaching begins with the admonition to go to your brother or sister who has wronged you and show them his or her fault. This teaching illustrates the first part of the forgiveness process: naming the wrong that has been done.

When someone has sinned against us, we can only begin the process of forgiveness once the wrong has been named. What exactly happened between the two parties? Who did what and how was it perceived? What were the feelings that it evoked? We can explore all of this when we "show our brother his fault."

The second part of this process is that the sin (not the person!) must be shamed. The wrongdoing must be declared a sin. The more specific this is, the better. For example, "when you lied to me about why you missed our meeting, it hurt me and that was not okay." Forgiveness begins when the sin involved is named and shamed.

It is important to remember here that all this is to be done in love. The goal of Jesus' instructions regarding forgiveness is reconciliation, not shaming someone who has done us wrong. Anyone who has hurt you should be approached with love and with a heart to reconcile. Then, when you "show them their fault" it can open a door to redemption and not burn the bridge between you.

✤ Is saying, "It's okay," part of authentic forgiveness? Why did you answer the way you did?

✤ What's the difference between shaming the sin that's been done by a person and shaming the person?

✤ Have you ever had someone show you your fault? How did it go? Did they do it well or poorly? What made it that way?

❖ Is it easy or hard for you to say when you've been wronged?
Explain your answer.

 # DAY 2

PSALM 103:11–12

> For as high as the heavens are above the earth,
> so great is his love for those who fear him;
> as far as the east is from the west,
> so far has he removed our transgressions from us.

Read the scripture for today and consider:

❖ When you hear that God loves those who "fear Him," what does
it mean to you?

If the first steps in forgiveness are naming and shaming the offense committed between the two parties, the next step is even more difficult. It involves sending away the offense and releasing the offender. Psalm 103 paints a picture of what God's forgiveness does to the connection between our sins and ourselves. He utterly separates them. They are removed as far as the east is from the west. This pattern of removal and sending away is exactly what happens when we forgive one another.

Once the offense has been named and shamed the offender is laid bare. Their sin is before them and the debt they have incurred from their neighbor is in their face. What happens next is a picture of God's grace. The offended releases the offender, saying, "I'm not going to make you pay for what you've done. I forgive you." This is, in effect, sending the sin away.

Sometimes this is something that happens one time and is done, but sometimes the offense has such consequences that release must happen over and over again in the heart of a person. This is all right because forgiveness is more of a process than an event. Also, sending the sin away means we do not keep dragging it up over and over again. Once we send it away the work becomes internal, but don't worry. God's Spirit will empower us to act in these powerful ways.

✤ Think of a time you have been forgiven for something by another person. Did it take a long time to work through? How did you feel afterward?

❖ Have you ever had someone repeatedly bring up something you did wrong? How did you handle it?

❖ What is the hardest part for you about letting go of an offense?

 # DAY 3

ROMANS 12:17–21

Do not repay anyone evil for evil. Be careful to do what is right in the eyes of everyone. If it is possible, as far as it depends on you, live at peace with everyone. Do not take revenge, my dear friends, but leave room for God's wrath, for it is written: "It is mine to avenge; I will repay," says the Lord.

Read the scripture for today and consider:

✣ Have you ever been tempted to take revenge on someone who hurt you?

✣ Have you ever taken revenge on someone? If so, what was the result?

✣ What does it mean to let God make it right when we've been wronged?

We have been tracking the process of forgiveness this week, starting with the need to name and shame the wrong that has been done, followed by the offender releasing the offended of their debt. This process makes up the bones of forgiveness. However, as with so many things, there are nuances to forgiveness and a big one is what to do if the person you are forgiving doesn't want your forgiveness. This takes us back to today's scripture.

Romans 12:17–21 records Paul counseling the church in Rome about how to deal with their conflicts. He challenges them in verse 18 to use all their power to live at peace with everyone. However, what if the person you have conflict with won't receive your peace? What if you've done everything in your power to live at peace with someone but it's still not enough? It is then that we remember the difference between forgiveness and reconciliation.

Reconciliation is the dream. It is the hope we carry that our broken relationships can be made whole. However, sometimes, because of the nature of the offence, reconciliation might be impossible or even dangerous. This does not mean that forgiveness is also impossible. It just changes the goal.

Reconciliation takes two people to accomplish. It requires that both offender and offended work together to forge a new and redeemed relationship. Forgiveness, on the other hand, only requires one person. It is something we can do whether anyone else participates or not.

✣ In your own words, what is the difference between forgiveness and reconciliation?

✣ What are three things you can do to "live at peace" with others?

✣ Is there anything you are doing that works against that?

 # DAY 4

ISAIAH 43:25

I, even I, am he who blots out
your transgressions, for my own sake,
and remembers your sins no more.

ISAIAH 64:9

Do not be angry beyond measure, LORD;
    do not remember our sins forever.
Oh, look on us, we pray,
    for we are all your people.

Read the scripture for today and consider:

✠ What do these two passages have in common (other than the author)?

The phrase "forgive and forget" never appears in the Bible, and for good reason. As much as forgiveness involves releasing those who have hurt us from the debt they incurred, sometimes we need to remember their sins. If you have forgiven someone who was abusive, neglectful, addicted, or threatened physical danger to you, you should not return to that relationship without reflection. Forgiveness does not require us to go back into a dangerous situation, which is why it is important to remember that forgiving and forgetting do not always go hand in hand.

However, as much as this is true, it is not the whole truth. Both of the texts we read today from Isaiah talk about how God will one day forget our sins. This will be the completion of our redemption. He will not only forgive us but also "remember our sins no more."

What that means for us today is simple. Because we live on this side of the renewal of all things, we must be wise when we forget. Our church communities can help us discern the best response in each situation. However, let's remember that there will be times when our forgiveness will actually yield forgetting. We may reconcile with a neighbor and not be able to remember what the fight was about a year later. This is a taste of what is to come and we should savor it.

✚ What's the difference between remembering sin to keep us safe and repeatedly bringing something up from the past?

✛ In your own words, why should you sometimes not "forgive and forget"?

 DAY 5

MATTHEW 6:14–15

For if you forgive other people when they sin against you, your heavenly Father will also forgive you. But if you do not forgive others their sins, your Father will not forgive your sins.

Read the scripture for today and consider:

✛ What do you think Jesus means when he says if you do not forgive others their sin, you will not be forgiven?

For this last reflection on forgiveness, let us look at the way forgiveness flows to us and from us. If you have ever been swimming underwater, you know what is like to hold your breath a bit too long and come quickly up for air. However, the first thing you have to do before you inhale oxygen is exhale the carbon dioxide from your lungs. It is not until you've done that, that you are able to take your next breath. They both flow through the same pipe.

This is how Jesus says forgiveness works in Matthew 6:14–15. Just as you have to exhale carbon dioxide before you can breathe in the oxygen, you must, says Jesus, be open to forgive others if you desire to be forgiven by God. Because the channel of forgiveness to others and forgiveness from God is the same place in our hearts, if we close one off, the other will be closed as well. This is not a punishment as much as it is a consequence. Jesus knows this is how humans were made to be, so he warns us not to suffocate in our unforgiveness. If we remain open to extending grace to others, the channel of God's grace to our hearts will remain wide open as well.

✤ Is there anyone you need to forgive?

✛ Is the channel of forgiveness to your heart more open or closed?

✛ Is it harder to receive God's grace yourself or extend grace to others?

THE RADICAL INDIVIDUAL
RUMORS OF COMMITMENT

Have you ever considered what the point of the church is? Your answer can have a big impact on what you might expect the relational dynamic to be when you walk through the doors of your local church. Does the church exist to serve my needs like a vending machine of religious goods and services, or does it exist for something else?

A few years ago some Christians began to address this question with a challenge: "Don't go to church; be the church." The missive was simple but really cut to the core of what we are called to as the family of God. Church is not simply a place that we go to, but it is a presence that we are. The church does not exist to serve the needs of its people but instead looks to partner with God by being the hands and feet of Jesus in the world. Darren and Jon tell some stories in this session that challenge us to look at what we think of the church, how we relate to it, and finally how we will be the hands and feet of Christ in our neighborhood, city, and world.

CHECKING IN

Last week's experiment in truth was to pray for someone who has hurt you or who you would consider your enemy. Reflect here or share with a group:

✤ If you could describe your experience with this exercise in three words, what would they be?

✤ Was this experiment easier or harder than you imagined?

✤ What did you learn about yourself through this exercise?

WATCH THE DVD

Play Session 5: *The Radical Individual: Rumors of Commitment*

GROUP DISCUSSION

1. Of what group or organization are you an official member? (Could be a church, fan club, book group, etc.)

2. Jon opens the session by telling a story about one of his parishioners who "didn't get anything out of the worship." What was your reaction to his story?

3. The guys explore the rise of the modern individual starting in World War II and continuing on into the present day. Do you agree with the way they put the story together? What do you or do you not connect with?

4. Did you resonate with the guys' take on how our culture defines men (James Bond, hero types) and women (Audrey Hepburn, sex symbols)? Where do you see these false ideals expressed today? If you don't agree, what do you see instead?

5. What are the ways our culture gets community and commitment right? What are they ways it does not?

6. When you hear the biblical phrase, "the body of Christ," how do you define it?

7. How does the maxim, "Don't go to church; be the church," relate to this session?

8. Brainstorm as a group: What are three ways you and/or your church community struggle with seeing the church as a place that caters to your needs? What are three ways your community can be the hands and feet of Christ in your neighborhood this week?

EXPERIMENTS IN TRUTH
FULFILL YOUR VOWS TO THE MOST HIGH

PSALM 50:14

> Sacrifice thank offerings to God,
> fulfill your vows to the Most High.

One of the central dynamics of the Christian life is fidelity. Fidelity is faithfulness to a commitment or cause, demonstrated by long and consistent devotion. God's faithfulness is demonstrated over and over again in the Scriptures and presents a challenge to those in the church today who desire to live in His image. How can we get better at faithfulness? The answer: we practice.

This week you are invited to make one promise or vow before God (and your community) and keep that promise throughout the entire week. It may be a promise of abstinence (giving up sugar for the week) or a vow of activism (I will empty the dishwasher every night this week without being asked). It can be a commitment of hospitality (inviting someone over for dinner) or community service (volunteering in your church nursery). Whatever you choose, make the vow as a way of saying yes to God and no to the consumer notions of Christianity that *Rumors of God* so deftly exposes. Run it by your group or a friend before you begin and keep notes about your experience to share next time.

DAY BY DAY

The invitation of *Rumors of God* is to let go of our self-centered, consumer-oriented ideas of what it is to be Christians and embrace God's rich invitation to the other-centered, service-oriented world-view of the kingdom of God. The reflections this week all deal with the nature and purpose of the church. It is the home in which we have been placed by Christ and the place that, through Him, we can call home.

 DAY 1

1 CORINTHIANS 6:19–20

Do you not know that your bodies are temples of the Holy Spirit, who is in you, whom you have received from God? You are not your own; you were bought at a price. Therefore honor God with your bodies.

Read the scripture for today and consider:

✤ In your own words, what do you think is the purpose of the church?

The scriptures for next two days are from the letter of 1 Corinthians. In both verses, Paul was responding to problems in the Corinthian church and calling them back to Christ by reminding them why the church existed in the first place.

In 1 Corinthians 6:19–20 Paul addresses issues of sexual immorality in the community. These were Greek people who thought that there was a hard division between body and spirit (not a biblical idea) and that only the spirit of a person mattered. Therefore, it didn't matter what a person did with their body (like sexual promiscuity), they thought, because it would not affect their immortal soul. Paul disagreed.

In response to these broken assumptions, Paul invoked the Jewish temple, telling the Corinthian church that their bodies were "temples of the Holy Spirit." The temple was the dwelling place of the Lord in Judaism. It was the meeting place of heaven and earth. Moreover, the Jews believed that the way God filled the first temple was a precursor to the way He would one day fill the entire creation. What happened in the temple announced to the world what God was like and what He would do.

By calling Corinthians' bodies "temples of God's spirit," Paul reminded them that they could not just do whatever they physically desired. God's reputation is at stake because the Spirit dwells *inside* each of you now. What you do with your body is an announcement about who God is and what God is up to. This begs the question: What do we announce about God with the way we treat our bodies?

✢ In your own words, what does it mean that our bodies are "the temple of the Holy Spirit"?

✢ What do you and your community announce about God with the way you treat your bodies?

 DAY 2
I CORINTHIANS 12:27

Now you are the body of Christ, and each one of you is a part of it.

Read the scripture for today and consider:

✦ When you hear the phrase "body of Christ," what do you think it means?

When God created the heavens and the earth, human beings were His final work. The man and the woman were given a very special designation; they were made in the image of God. This description has less to do with physicality than with vocation. As God's image bearers, they have a job to do. They were created, according to Genesis 1 and 2, to *image* God in the creation. This means they are to demonstrate with their lives what God is like and they are to execute any tasks that God wants done in His creation. This is what it is to image God.

Paul drew on this concept when he reminded the Corinthians that they were the "body of Christ." When Jesus was born of the Virgin

Mary, He was God's image bearer par excellence. He perfectly demonstrated what true humanity looks like. However, He passed that job onto his disciples. This is what Paul wanted the Corinthians to remember.

In this church racked with in-fighting and all manner of carnality, Paul dared them to remember their purpose: *You all have a job to do. You can't live like this, because then you are saying something untrue about God. You all, together, are the body of Christ!* This challenges us to ask, what do we say about God with how our church communities live together?

✠ What does it mean to you to be part of the "body of Christ"?

✠ What are our churches most known for? Is this good or bad?

✢ What are three things your community announces about God based on how you live among one another?

 ## DAY 3

1 CORINTHIANS 12:12–19

Just as a body, though one, has many parts, but all its many parts form one body, so it is with Christ. For we were all baptized by one Spirit so as to form one body—whether Jews or Gentiles, slave or free—and we were all given the one Spirit to drink. Even so the body is not made up of one part but of many.

Now if the foot should say, "Because I am not a hand, I do not belong to the body," it would not for that reason stop being part of the body. And if the ear should say, "Because I am not an eye, I do not belong to the body," it would not for that reason stop being part of the body. If the whole body were an eye, where would the sense of hearing be? If the whole body were an ear, where would the sense of smell be? But in fact God has placed the parts in the body, every one of them, just as he wanted them to be. If they were all one part, where would the body be? As it is, there are many parts, but one body.

Read the scripture for today and consider:

✛ In your own words, what do you think is the point of the body metaphor above?

When you talk to people who go to church, things always get uncomfortable when you discuss money and membership. It is the latter that might surprise some of you, but it's true. People today are very hesitant to join up and commit themselves to anything. They are much more comfortable with keeping their options open than planting their flag and declaring that they belong to any one church.

In 1 Corinthians 12:12–19, Paul challenged the Corinthians to stop seeking status based on spiritual gifts. Everyone is important in the church, and because everyone has a different part to play, we cannot elevate one set of gifts over another. The great public speaker is not more important than the group that makes the coffee. The Corinthians had forgotten that truth and Paul reminded them how much they needed each other.

Perhaps the application of this scripture extends to our coyness when it comes to committing to a community of faith. Somewhere, somehow, we really do believe we can say to the hand of the church,

"I don't need you," but that statement is just not true. We do need each other, and though devotion to a particular community can be challenging, it will grow in us the fruit of the spirit. Let us today have the courage to belong to the body.

✤ How does your church or faith community do membership?

✤ Are you a member of your church? Why or why not?

✤ What gifts of your own do you share with your church? Do you feel they are valued? Why or why not?

 DAY 4

I CORINTHIANS 8:9–13

Be careful, however, that the exercise of your rights does not become a stumbling block to the weak. For if someone with a weak conscience sees you, with all your knowledge, eating in an idol's temple, won't that person be emboldened to eat what is sacrificed to idols? So this weak brother or sister, for whom Christ died, is destroyed by your knowledge. When you sin against them in this way and wound their weak conscience, you sin against Christ. Therefore, if what I eat causes my brother or sister to fall into sin, I will never eat meat again, so that I will not cause them to fall.

Read the scripture for today and consider:

✤ What is something that stood out to you from the reading this morning?

In the ancient world, eating meat was a luxury. The opportunity to eat it did not come up often, and when it did in Corinth, it was usually because an animal had been sacrificed to a pagan deity. Paul had already established, earlier in the letter, that eating such "idol meat" was not sinful in and of itself. According to Paul, the gods it had been offered to were not real, so it did no harm to eat the sacrificed meat. There was a way this meat was harmful to the community, however, which is what today's scripture reading addresses.

Most of the new members of the Corinthian church had converted out of one of these old pagan religions. Yet when they saw their seasoned church leaders eating this "idol meat," it was confusing. Did this mean they could worship their old gods and not Jesus alone?

Recognizing this dynamic in addition to the leadership's unwillingness to give up the practice, Paul called them all back to what mattered.

Even though the older Christians considered themselves "strong" (read a little sarcasm here) enough to eat meat, it was not so for the "weak" among them. Therefore, Paul advised the strong to give up their right to indulge in the luxury of meat for the sake of the weak. Not because it was wrong to eat it but as an act of love.

✠ What do you think are some contemporary parallels to the "idol meat" issue for the church in our time?

✤ How is giving up your rights to something an act of love?

✤ Can you think of a time when it was easy to give up your rights? How about a time when it was difficult?

 ## DAY 5

COLOSSIANS 3:5–11

Put to death, therefore, whatever belongs to your earthly nature: sexual immorality, impurity, lust, evil desires and greed, which is idolatry. Because of these, the wrath of God is coming. You used to walk in these ways, in the life you once lived. But now you must also rid yourselves of all such things as these: anger, rage, malice, slander, and filthy language from your lips. Do not lie to each other, since you have taken off your old self with its practices and have put on the new self, which is being renewed in knowledge in the image of its Creator. Here there is no Gentile or Jew, circumcised or uncircumcised, barbarian, Scythian, slave or free, but Christ is all, and is in all.

Read the scripture for today and consider:

✤ Verse 5 says, "Put to death, therefore, whatever belongs to your earthly nature: sexual immorality, impurity, lust, evil desires and greed, which is idolatry." How do you think greed is connected to idolatry?

When we say yes to Jesus' invitation to follow Him, we must invariably say no to other things. Anything that competes with God's kingdom or asks for our allegiance to something other than Jesus has to be reevaluated and sometimes outright rejected.

This was the issue the church in Colossae faced. They were a diverse community with many different social, political, economic, and ethnic backgrounds. Apparently, the members of the church kept bringing the old divisions, battles, and prejudices of the different backgrounds into the church. This dynamic was destroying the unity of the Colossian church and compromising their existence and mission.

Colossians 3 addressed this situation directly by shifting everyone's perspective. The cultures found in the Colossian church were not inherently bad. In fact, they were a gift from God. However, that gift becomes distorted when it is used to cause discord and alienation. This is why verse 11 proclaims that the church is a place where the old divisions of the world (represented here by all the ethnic, religious, social, and economic dichotomies that follow) are given no harbor. We have left those things behind and have a new identity in Christ. This means saying yes to Jesus and saying no to anything (even good things) that bend us away from His light.

✛ Can you think of any parallels between the Colossian church and our church today? What are some of the divisions of the world that we import into the church?

✛ Is there a cultural divide you recognize that you hold onto some- times? If so what is it?

✤ Is there anything you are being called to say no to so you can say yes to Jesus?

OUR BURNING REVOLUTION
RUMORS OF HOPE

If you ask people today to discuss who inspires them, they usually name someone who has accomplished something notable. It may be a captain of industry, a successful politician, a pioneer of technology, or an influential artist. Rarely does anyone seek inspiration in the lives of those who have failed, given up, or remained obscure, because our culture doesn't value those things. Our world today celebrates the exceptional and the leaders, leaving everyone else on the sidelines.

Jesus sees things differently.

From the time He called his first disciples to the moments when he empowered them after His resurrection, Jesus never picked the best and brightest by the world's standards. In fact, He did just the opposite. Jesus picked the average students, the passed over, and the discredited. He looked to build His kingdom with the hands and feet of men and women who betrayed Him, were disappointed by Him, and even denied Him. In short, Jesus chose people like us.

As opposed to our culture, which celebrates the accomplished, successful, and famous, Jesus bet it all on the washouts, failures, and obscure. He saw in them the potential to build God's new world and He sees it in us too. That's right; Jesus believes in us. He believes that with His power moving through us and filling our lungs (He breathed the Holy Spirit on the disciples, after all) we can make a new world together.

This week, consider whether this all sounds like good news to you, and if it does, decide whether you will take Jesus up on His invitation to bring God's kingdom here on earth as it is in heaven. Will you live out your faith in a way that tells everyone that the rumors of God are, in fact, true?

CHECKING IN

Last week's experiment in truth was to make a vow and keep it as a spiritual discipline. Reflect personally or with a group:

✚ What was your vow, and did you keep it? Why or why not?

✚ What did you learn about yourself through this exercise?

WATCH THE DVD

Play Session 6: *Our Burning Revolution: Rumors of Hope*

GROUP DISCUSSION

1. What has been the most challenging part of this small group experience? What has been the most rewarding?

2. The guys suggest that the way Jesus spent his forty days on earth between the resurrection and ascension says more about the heart of God than almost anything in the Scriptures. What do you think Jesus' choices reveal about God's character and kingdom?

3. Does the fact that Jesus chooses the dropouts, failures, and the obscure sound like good news to you? Why or why not?

4. The two disciples that Jesus met on the road to Emmaus are described as having been disappointed with how life had turned out, and that's where Jesus encountered them. Have you ever felt that way? Do you feel like Jesus met you in that place? Why or why not?

5. Have you ever felt like there was something that would disqualify you from being chosen by God? If so, what did you do as a result of that feeling?

6. What is one gift or talent you have that can be part of building God's new world?

7. Brainstorm as a group one practical thing that everyone can do to cultivate hope after this study concludes.

8. What is one thing you will take with you from this small group experience that will show the world that the rumors of God are true?

EXPERIMENTS IN TRUTH
SOMETHING BEAUTIFUL

Rumors of God takes Jesus' invitation to a different kind of life seriously. The authors then ask the hard question: How have things turned out since you accepted that invitation? Have things gone as you expected, and what might be the reasons for that?

Our last experiment in truth is an act of hope. In the face of our disappointment, cynicism, and fear, hope is a precious gift that must be nurtured. That is what this exercise is designed to do.

Grab a current newspaper or magazine, or go to an online news source. Read through the content and find a story that makes you feel hopeless, cynical, or afraid. Then, as an act of prayer, take a pair of scissors, cut out words and phrases from the article, and refashion them as a prayer. Make it a prayer that moves in the opposite spirit of the feeling the article evoked in you. Then, take a piece of paper and glue your prayer in place so you can look at it all week. Pray it as an act of hope. God has not given up on this world or on us, and neither should we.

Now pray, for God is near.

DAY BY DAY

Jesus' resurrection is the sign that death is defeated, the battle is over, and God's new world is emerging in the midst of our own. It is ground zero for Christian hope. The reflections this week ask us to look at how others in the Scriptures have addressed this hope and responded to God's new world both before and after Jesus' resurrection.

 # DAY 1

MATTHEW 28:11–15

While the women were on their way, some of the guards went into the city and reported to the chief priests everything that had happened. When the chief priests had met with the elders and devised a plan, they gave the soldiers a large sum of money, telling them, "You are to say, 'His disciples came during the night and stole him away while we were asleep.' If this report gets to the governor, we will satisfy him and keep you out of trouble." So the soldiers took the money and did as they were instructed. And this story has been widely circulated among the Jews to this very day.

Read the scripture for today and consider:

✚ Why do you think the chief priests and elders bribed the soldiers to lie about Jesus' resurrection?

Jesus' resurrection is the sign and marker that God's new world has begun. The Gospels communicate this in a variety of ways, not the least of which is by reminding us that Jesus was raised on the first day of the week and met Mary in a garden. These are two callbacks to the Genesis creation story and a way of showing that God's *new* creation is starting!

However, as Matthew's gospel shows us in chapter 28, this was not good news to everyone. The power brokers and religious leaders of the day were threatened by Jesus' resurrection. Not simply because it meant that Jesus was right and they were wrong but also because they were committed to the old order of things. They had carved out space in the world's broken system to get money, influence, and power for themselves and it was working for them to some degree. For Jesus to threaten to overturn that, well, it was just too much. So they created a story. They tried to sow misinformation about the truth of God's power.

We must ask ourselves if we do the same thing. Are we tempted to deny Jesus' resurrection by staying committed to the values, dreams, and stories of the old order? Do we have the courage to surrender ourselves and our dreams to God's new world? Only one of these worlds will endure. Which will you choose?

✤ In what way does God's new world order seem threatening to you?

✜ Is there any way that the old order of things works for you? How so?

✜ Are you ever tempted to "deny Jesus' resurrection" by pretending God's new world is not here? How so?

DAY 2

JOB 17:14–16

If I say to corruption, "You are my father,"
and to the worm, "My mother" or "My sister,"
where then is my hope—
who can see any hope for me?
Will it go down to the gates of death?
Will we descend together into the dust?

Read the scripture for today and consider:

+ How do Job's words sound to you? What do you think he is feeling?

Today's reading is a pretty bleak passage from the book of Job. In the text Job wonders if there is any hope for him. Everything looks grim. Corruption and the worm (two graphic images associated with a decomposing body) are his parents! "Where is my hope?" he cries out. If death is upon me, what am I hoping for? Is there anything more than this?

Perhaps you have felt this way. Perhaps there was a time when all you could see was darkness, when the light was dim at best and it seemed that death was a companion. No one is immune from such despair, but we can learn from Job about what to do in the midst of it.

Look at who Job was talking to in the text. He was talking to the Lord! From his despair, pain, and despondency he engaged in a sincere act of hope—he actually cried out to God. He was keeping the conversation going. Sometimes this is all we can do, and yet it is enough. The Spirit of God sustains our faith in the dark times and God will answer when we call. It may not look like what we expect, but we should call out indeed. The Lord is with us even in our hopelessness.

✤ Have you ever felt like Job did in this passage?

✤ How do you deal with the dark times in your life?

✤ What do you think it looks like for God to be with us in our hopelessness?

 # DAY 3

PSALM 71:1–6

In you, LORD, I have taken refuge;
  let me never be put to shame.
In your righteousness, rescue me and deliver me;
  turn your ear to me and save me.
Be my rock of refuge,
  to which I can always go;
give the command to save me,
  for you are my rock and my fortress.
Deliver me, my God, from the hand of the wicked,
  from the grasp of those who are evil and cruel.
For you have been my hope, Sovereign LORD,
  my confidence since my youth.
From birth I have relied on you;
  you brought me forth from my mother's womb.
  I will ever praise you.

Read the scripture for today and consider:

✛ What kind of circumstances do you think would inspire a psalm like this?

Have you ever had one of those days when everything just seemed to be going wrong? Has someone ever been out to get you? Have you ever found your life crashing down around you for no reason? If the answer is yes, then Psalm 71 is for you.

Psalm 71:1–6 is a deep appeal for rescue from God in the midst of one of life's storms. Whether the storm is big or little doesn't matter, because the admonition is the same: trust God for rescue. This is the picture of hope the psalm gives us.

However, before we imagine that this hope is mostly a mental exercise, we have to observe that there is something active the psalmist is doing. The psalmist is abstaining from revenge. In asking for deliverance from those who are evil and cruel, the psalmist decides not to fight fire with fire but instead calls out to God for rescue. He does this because he has hope. Hope that God really is who He claims to be and that God can and will act on his behalf. What do we believe when the chips are down?

✤ Think of a time when life was stormy. Did you find God in the storm? Why or why not?

❖ Is it easy or hard to hope that God will care for you when the going gets tough?

❖ Write a brief prayer for deliverance for that stormy season of life you mentioned before. Keep it somewhere and pull it out the next time things get hard.

 # DAY 4

Hopes placed in mortals die with them;
all the promise of their power comes to nothing

Read the scripture for today and consider:

✚ Can you think of an example from the Bible where this proverb would apply?

Security is a big deal and an even bigger business in the United States. From airport screenings to alarm systems at the mall we are hard at work building technology to help us avert tragedy. However, the problem is this is ultimately futile. No matter how carefully we plan and how cautiously we live, none of us can avoid risk and danger entirely. Which takes us back to the question the proverb is asking: Where do you put your trust?

There are lots of businesses, politicians, and community groups that will say, "Put your trust here!" However, as Christians, we know that wisdom instructs us to put our hope in God alone. This is what the proverb is reminding us. No person, ideology, or government can provide true security. Only God can. Trusting God doesn't guarantee that nothing bad will ever happen to us, but it does mean we can trust God to be with us when tragedy occurs. Only He can promise that, which is why if we put our hope in anything but the living God, our hopes will not last.

✠ Is there anywhere in your life you are tempted to trust something other than God for your security?

✠ What's the difference between putting your hope in God and being irresponsible or foolish with your choices?

✤ Does trusting in God mean that nothing bad will ever happen to you? Why or why not?

 DAY 5

MATTHEW 19:28

Jesus said to them, "Truly I tell you, at the renewal of all things, when the Son of Man sits on his glorious throne, you who have followed me will also sit on twelve thrones, judging the twelve tribes of Israel."

ACTS 3:21

Heaven must receive him until the time comes for God to restore everything, as he promised long ago through his holy prophets.

COLOSSIANS 1:19-20

For God was pleased to have all his fullness dwell in him, and through him to reconcile to himself all things, whether things on earth or things in heaven, by making peace through his blood, shed on the cross.

REVELATION 21:5a

He who was seated on the throne said, "I am making everything new!"

Read the scripture for today and consider:

✜ Can you find the common thread in each of the verses above and on the previous page?

For this, the last devotional of the series, we want to think about where everything is going. What is God's agenda on the earth? What context do we have for hope? The answer is found among the four texts listed above. Christian hope is anchored in a promise made by God thousands of years ago. It is a promise to heal this broken world and to put everything that is broken back together. The Jews described this agenda as *Tikkun Olam*, which translates loosely to "Fix Everything," which is indeed what God is doing.

The verses above show a few places where Jesus, His disciples, and later the church pick up and carry this promise. God really is healing this place. The vision of Revelation 21:5 really is where all this is going. This can be hard to hold onto, especially in the face of grief and tragedy, but it is true nonetheless. God really is renewing the whole creation. How can we do our part to join with God in this wonderful work?

✤ Do you see examples of God's renewing work in the world today? If so, where?

✤ What do you see and experience that makes *Tikkun Olam* hard to believe?

✤ Can you think of one place you are partnering with God to restore things even now? If so, where? If not, where can you start?

NOTES

1. Richard Rohr, *Breathing Under Water: Spirituality and the Twelve Steps* (Cincinnati: St. Anthony Messenger Press, 2011).

2. Irvin Kershner, Mark Hamill, Billy Dee Williams, Alec Guinness, Gary Kurtz, John Williams, Harrison Ford, et al., *Star Wars IV: A New Hope*, written and directed by George Lucas (Beverly Hills: 20th Century Fox Entertainment, 2004), DVD.

3. Brad H. Young, *The Parables: Jewish Interpretation and Christian Tradition* (repr., Grand Rapids, Baker Academic, 2008)

4. C. S. Lewis, *Mere Christianity: A Revised and Amplified Edition, with a New Introduction, of the Three Books,* Broadcast Talks, Christian Behaviour, *and* Beyond Personality (San Francisco: HarperSanFrancisco, 2011).

5. R. M. French, trans., *The Way of a Pilgrim: and The Pilgrim Continues His Way* (1884 repr., San Francisco: Harper, 1991)

DARREN WHITEHEAD AND JON TYSON

RUMORS OF GOD

FORWARD BY BILL HYBELS

This world is a great sculptor's shop
and we are the statues.
But there is a rumor going round the shop
that some of us are
some day going to come to life.

C.S. LEWIS

DARREN WHITEHEAD & JON TYSON

RUMORS OF GOD

EXPERIENCE THE KIND OF FAITH YOU'VE ONLY HEARD ABOUT

FOREWORD BY BILL HYBELS